To:

....

From:

....

Like arrows
in the hands of a warrior are the
children born when a man is young.
Blessed is the father whose
quiver is full of them.

Adapted from Psalm 127:4-6

For Dad from a Thankful Heart
Copyright 1998 by ZondervanPublishingHouse

ISBN 0-310-97686-3

Senior Editor: Gwen Ellis
Designed by: Left Coast Design, Inc.
Compiled by: Jean E. Syswerda

Published by

ZondervanPublishingHouse

Grand Rapids, MI 49530, U.S.A.
http://www.zondervan.com

Printed in China.

98 99 00 01 02/HK/12 11 10 9 8 7 6 5 4 3 2 1

for Dad

From a
Thankful Heart

Zondervan*Gifts*

We have a gift for inspiration™

The potential
possibilities of any child
are the most intriguing and
stimulating in all creation.

RAY L. WILBUR

R ise up, O men of God!
Have done with lesser things.
Give heart and mind and soul and
strength
To serve the King of kings.

Rise up, O men of God!
The kingdom tarries long.
Bring in the day of brotherhood
And end the night of wrong.

Rise up, O men of God!
The church for you doth wait,
Her strength unequal to her task;
Rise up and make her great!

Lift high the cross of Christ!
Tread where His feet have trod.
As brothers of the Son of Man,
Rise up, O men of God!

WILLIAM P. MERRILL

We laughed loud and long in our family, and I am convinced that our sense of play has held us together during difficult times. I know that my father's intuitive understanding of the need for recess is one of the reasons why I loved him so much when I was a boy. My dad celebrates life and takes everybody near him along for the ride if they will hang on.

JACK & JERRY SCHREUR

Praise be to the LORD, who has given rest to his people Israel just as he promised. Not one word has failed of all the good promises he gave through his servant Moses. May the LORD our God be with us as he was with our fathers; may he never leave us nor forsake us. May he turn our hearts to him, to walk in all his ways and to keep the commands, decrees and regulations he gave our fathers. And may these words of mine, which I have prayed before the LORD, be near to the LORD our God day and night, that he may uphold the cause of his servant and the cause of his people Israel according to each day's need, so that all the peoples of the earth may know that the LORD is God and that there is no other. But your hearts must be fully committed to the LORD our God, to live by his decrees and obey his commands, as at this time."

KING SOLOMON
1 KINGS 8:56-61

And because he was there life went smoothly. The car always ran, the bills got paid, and the lawn stayed mowed. Because he was there the laughter was fresh and the future was secure. Because he was there my growing up was what God intended growing up to be; a storybook scamper through the magic and mystery of the world.

Because he was there we kids never worried about things like income tax, savings accounts, monthly bills or mortgages. Those were the things on Daddy's desk.

We have lots of family pictures without him. Not because he wasn't there, but because he was always behind the camera.

He made the decisions, broke up the fights, chuckled at Archie Bunker, read the paper every evening, and fixed breakfast on Sundays. He didn't do anything unusual. He only did what dads are supposed to do—be there.

MAX LUCADO

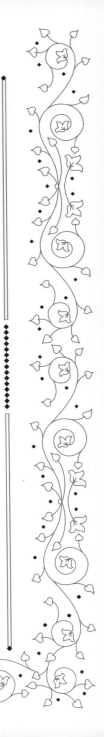

It was a warm spring morning, and we were returning from the daily chore of slopping the pigs and feeding the other animals. It was the most unexpected question I'd ever heard from him. Walking up Randolph Hill, the only road that led back to our house, my dad asked, "Lonnie, want to race?"

Well, I considered myself pretty fast in those days. I also had a reputation for never turning down a challenge. But race my dad? "What if I beat him?" I thought to myself. "Boy, if I beat him, I might be slopping those pigs alone for the next ten years! Or, worse yet, what if he beats me? What would I say to my friends? Or what if this old guy suddenly keeled over after inhaling the cloud of dust—my trademark at takeoff? After all he must be twenty-five years old! He could have a heart attack! Mom would never forgive me. In a few short minutes, I could be fatherless and Mom could be without a husband."

I regained my composure and looked up at him with a kind of smugness in my smile and thought, "Lonnie, this man has challenged you—and that's that!"

Then, before I knew what was happening, he interrupted my thoughts with his words. He shouted them quickly, almost as though he were trying to get an edge by catching me off guard. "Ready, set, go!" And we were off.

In the distance, I could see Mom as she stepped out of the back door of our house, her hands waving in the morning sun as though she were cheering for her favorite team. Oh, it was nip and tuck, neck and neck for the first few yards. But soon it was all over.

The next thing I remember is the three of us lying in the yard gasping for air and laughing so hard that tears ran down our faces. Dad's laughter was probably due to the fact that it had been some time since he had run thirty yards like that! Mom gathered the both of us up in her arms, laughing and enjoying the fun of being together. My laughter came from the discovery that my dad could run—he really could run!

When I had kids of my own, I realized another reason why this memory is special. It was a moment very typical of my parents. Dad and Mom, though busy always making ends meet and dealing with all that grown-ups have to be concerned with, often took time to be involved in my little world.

Oh, who won the race? It didn't matter.

LARNELLE HARRIS

What does your presence say? It says, "You are so important that I want to be with you." Parents, build friendships through your person presence.

V. GILBERT BEERS

In a discussion about fathering, noted author, pastor and teacher Dr. Charles Swindoll commented on what he would do differently as a father if he could do it over again. His first response was simple and worth taking to heart: "I would say 'YES' more often!"

PAUL LEWIS

I will lean over her carriage and go "Hi." She will smile up at me—that much, there is no imagining. I will say it again. Still the smile. I will say it still again. And . . . something audible will come forth from her. It's nowhere close to a human word, but it is her trying to return whatever it is I am signaling to her.

I guess the thing that surprises me the most is that this should move me so much. Before, I was a little puzzled by the big deal people made over their babies' first words—the concept seemed so normal, so routine. And there I am, gazing in wonderment because she will try so hard to make a noise to match mine.

My wife Susan thinks it's a case of Amanda being advanced. But I think it's just another case of us being swept away by miracles we were never even aware of.

BOB GREENE

> *When you become a parent it is your biggest chance to grow again. You have another crack at yourself.*
>
> **FRED ROGERS**
> *"Mr. Rogers"*

F*athers, do not*
exasperate your children; instead,
bring them up in the training
and instruction of the Lord.

EPHESIANS 6:4

In a dad's world of adult pressures, it's easy to forget how to abandon yourself to the moment—to truly "play!" So, Dad, take a short class from your "midget gurus of play." Watch how they do it, then join in for a "lab session."

PAUL LEWIS

Words have an awesome impact. The impression made by a father's voice can set in motion an entire trend of life.
GORDON MACDONALD

Govern a small family as you would cook a small fish, gently.
CHINESE PROVERB

It is better to bind your child to you by a feeling of respect and by gentleness, than by fear.
TERENCE

I believe that I'm letting my kids see that a man can be tender, sensible, warm, attentive to feelings, and present, just plain there. That's important to me, because I didn't get any of that from my own father, and I am realizing now how much I missed it.
ANONYMOUS

By profession I am a soldier and take pride in that fact. But I am prouder— infinitely prouder—to be a father.
DOUGLAS MACARTHUR

Don't limit a child to your own learning, for he was born in another time.
JEWISH PROVERB

In a Christian father a child ought to have a better exposition than the best of sermons can give of the love and care of the heavenly Father and all the blessing and joy He wants to bestow.

But to attain to this the parent must consciously and distinctly aim at making himself and the name he bears the ladder by which the child can climb to the Father above. It is when the bright, living, happy piety of the parents, a

mingling of holy reverence to God with childlike love, shines on the children from their early youth that the name of God as Father will become linked with all that is lovely and holy in the manner of a child. It is not so much a matter of reflection or thought but as the life-breath taken in all unconsciously that the fatherhood of earth will have been the gate of the Father's home above.

And is it possible so to live that all this shall be true? The one thing the Father loves to give, the sum and center of all His good gifts, is His own Holy Spirit—His Father-Spirit to be in us. And we have but to believe, and as we believe, to receive, and as we receive, to yield to and live in the Spirit, and He will make our fatherhood the image of God's, and from us, too, there will flow streams of living water to bless our children.

ANDREW MURRAY

O my people,
    hear my teaching;
listen to the words of my mouth.

I will open my mouth in parables,
    I will utter hidden things, things from of
    old—

what we have heard and known,
    what our fathers have told us.

We will not hide them from their children;
    we will tell the next generation
the praiseworthy deeds of the LORD,
    his power, and the wonders he has done.

He decreed statutes for Jacob
    and established the law in Israel,
which he commanded our forefathers
    to teach their children,

so the next generation would know them,
    even the children yet to be born,
    and they in turn would tell their children.

Then they would put their trust in God
    and would not forget his deeds
    but would keep his commands.

PSALM 78:1-7

One image of my father sticks with me from my youth. I was only about nine years old when Dad took me to downtown Chicago to the Pacific Garden Mission. I had never been to a mission before, and I was scared to death. The place was filled with smelly, filthy, loud men, people I had never been in contact with before. In my sanitized world there were good people. They had jobs, took baths, got married, and went to church. And there were bad people. They lived on the street, drank alcohol, smoked cigarettes, didn't have jobs, and never went to church. Such is the mind of a nine-year-old. These men were so bad according to my calculations that they were off the scale. I don't remember much of what happened that evening. I just have an image of my dad with his arm around a lice-infested man who reeked of liquor and garbage, telling him that Jesus loved him. My sanitized version of the world was knocked completely out of whack. There was my clean-cut pastor father, touching a "bad" man.

I learned a lot about Jesus that night. I learned a lot about the Gospel. I learned a lot about forgiveness. And I learned a lot about my father.

JACK & JERRY SCHREUR

Sometimes the smallest things almost break my heart.

When my baby daughter Amanda is startled, she smiles. There will be a sudden noise from outside; or I will walk into the room unexpectedly; or the phone will ring.

And she will turn her head toward the direction of the intrusion, and her immediate instinct will be to grin that toothless grin. It is as if she believes that whatever comes into her world, it is bound to be pleasant and happy. It does not occur to her that anything might harm her; every signal she has received so far has told her that whatever happens will be good.

And of course that will not always be so. The day will come when she learns to be wary; when she learns not to trust anything she does not know. I think about that when I see her jerk her head and smile; I make myself pay attention, for soon enough she will have changed.

I thought it was just me noticing this. But tonight Susan was staring at Amanda as she laughed; Susan said, "It's so sad. She's eventually going to have to learn that the world can be awful."

I guess that's right. But for now, we can watch her face light up.

BOB GREENE

I have observed that the greatest delusion is to suppose that our children will be devout Christians simply because their parents have been or that any of them will enter into the Christian faith in any other way than through their parents' deep travail of prayer and faith. But this prayer demands time, time that cannot be given if it is all signed and conscripted and laid on the altar of career ambition. Failure for you at this point would make mere success in your occupation a very pale and washed-out affair indeed.

JAMES C. DOBSON, SR.

I always loved him, that great big hulk of a man who once carried an upright piano on his back, but yet could hold a kitten with more gentleness than its own mother. He was fair, honest, strict, tender, strong, and had a deep sense of right and wrong born of a genuine love for God.

I remember so many things about him. We'd cut wood for our stoves in the fall of the year and he'd invite me to come. It was a special time for me to be alone with him. We'd plant potatoes in the spring—he digging the holes and me dropping the potatoes into the holes and covering them. When we went ice skating, he'd spend all his time clearing the ice of snow so that we could spin with great abandon. Or if we were sledding, he'd drive his truck up and down the hill to pack the snow and make the sled run slick. He was always trying to make things better for us. And he could be sillier than almost anyone I've ever known.

But most of all I'd remember the tears in his eyes as he'd talk about his Lord and Savior Jesus Christ. He'd tell us about that night long ago when he had a vision and God became more than a word to him. About how his surrender to God had completely changed his life forever.

I love him very much, for you see, he was and is my daddy.

GWEN ELLIS

Last year, I spoke to seven hundred high school students about the importance of making amends with others. A sixteen-year-old boy moved close, looked around to see if anyone was listening, and said quietly, "My dad left us when I was a little kid. Who is going to teach me to be a man?" He began to cry. "I mess up every relationship I get into. I hurt the people I care the most about. I really hurt this girl. I need to make it right but I don't know how. Who's going to teach me how to relate to people?" The day that young man's dad walked away (for whatever reason), he sentenced his son to years, perhaps a lifetime, of trying to figure out how to relate to people.

According to the apostle Paul and the Bible, dads are responsible for the social condition of their children. Instead of exasperating children by being absentee or abusive fathers, we must equip children practically, positionally, and personally.

How can dads fulfill this incredibly difficult role? The answer lies in Paul's words, "in the instruction of the Lord" (Ephesians 6:4). We need divine assistance in order to be people of faith—and good fathers.

DAVID MOORE

*The living,
the living—they praise you,
as I am doing today;
fathers tell their children
about your faithfulness.*

*The LORD will save me,
and we will sing with stringed
    instruments
all the days of our lives
in the temple of the LORD.*

ISAIAH 38:19-20

It struck me that some of the catchy little phrases that I like to use in seminars were coming back to haunt me, especially "Love them and let them go." I didn't want to let Holly go to college. Something kept telling me to turn that car around and go back and get her and take her home with us. I wanted to tell her, "You're not all grown up yet. We want you back. We need you back!"

I knew it was silly, of course. Our daughter was grown up, and it was time to get out of the nest and find out what that self-image we had all been working on for eighteen years was made of.

And then I thought back over those eighteen years—all the way back to that first chilly night in November when we brought her home from the hospital. . . . The awesome responsibility of being father to this twenty-and-one-half-inch little being had hit me hard. I was charged with shaping and molding the kind of young woman she would become some day. . . .

As I drove along, I remembered one of my favorite pieces of advice to new parents: "Start leaving your child with a babysitter as

> *I don't know who my grandfather was; I'm much more concerned to know what his grandson will be.*
>
> ABRAHAM LINCOLN

young as two weeks. Be sure to get out with your wife and work on your marriage. . . ."

Yes, that's what I tell them and I'm convinced it's true, but that didn't make it any easier to leave my daughter behind.

I realize that my firstborn daughter had often been right and I had often been wrong. The father, psychologist, and counselor had sat at the feet of his child and had learned important lessons of his own. And now she had gone off to school to study and learn—and grow even further away from us, as she should, of course. Things would never be quite the same again. Our relationship to Holly had now changed. The parent/child "umbilical cord" had been cut and she was on her own, totally responsible for everything, from brushing her teeth to paying her bills.

If you're a younger parent who still has younger children—particularly the ankle-biter type who never gives you a moment's peace—you may be wondering, "What's wrong with you, Leman? Why all this fuss about a daughter moving out of the house? I can't wait until that day. I wish I could have just one afternoon alone—even an hour's peace."

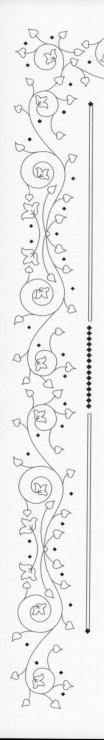

I can remember saying the same thing. But the day will come when those little ones will be "all grown up" and then the bottom line questions will be:

Did we build a strong, loving relationship with our children?

Did we raise adults who are responsible and ready to take on the world?

Did we bring our kids up without tearing them down?

I hope your answer is a big yes to all three questions.

KEVIN LEMAN

Family life is too intimate to be preserved by the spirit of justice. It can be sustained by a spirit of love, which goes beyond justice.

REINHOLD NIEBUHR

I t's not the quantity but the quality of time that really counts."

On the surface, this concept seems to make a lot of sense. It is possible to spend much time with one's family that is seemingly meaningless. All of us experience times when we are at home physically but our minds are wandering miles away. I can remember days with the family that could have been "scratched" in terms of "quality."

So what is the "quality time" myth? It's as phony as the fake diamond in a one-dollar ring; it's the rationale that allows people like me to relieve a guilty conscience while we go on neglecting our responsibility as a parent. The fact is, there is no quality without quantity.

DAVID JEREMIAH

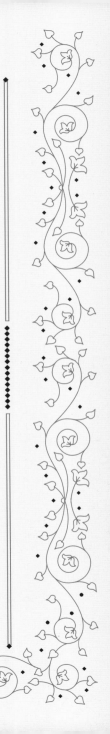

It's so easy for fatherhood to become a side issue in our lives, something we can spend some time on if and when we get a spare hour. If a paycheck came in each week for fatherhood, though, we'd all feel obligated to stay current with the family scene, to be on top of things at home. I'm certainly not advocating tax-supported pay for fatherhood. On the contrary, I'd suggest that we all recognize that we are being paid for fatherhood. It's not a dollars-and-cents proposition, and it doesn't come in regular installments with periodic increases. It comes whenever our kids laugh, whenever they jump on us with unsolicited hugs.

S. ADAMS SULLIVAN

Love the LORD your God with all your heart and with all your soul and with all your strength. These commandments that I give you today are to be upon your hearts. Impress them on your children. Talk about them when you sit at home and when you walk along the road, when you lie down and when you get up.

DEUTERONOMY 6:5-7

When each of our children was born, we thought of that child as 1) a full, complete person, and 2) someone equal to us in God's eyes. We never viewed our child as only part of a person, less than a person, or someone who would emerge into personhood. Each child was always a person, a full person, a complete person. We began thinking that way as soon as we knew that Arlie was pregnant. There was a person, although an unknown person, growing in her. At birth that person broke upon our horizon with all the attributes of personhood. Now the child had a face, a body we could cuddle and feed, a personality, a name.

V. GILBERT BEERS

J esus continued:
"There was a man who had two sons. The younger one said to his father, 'Father, give me my share of the estate.' So he divided his property between them.

"Not long after that, the younger son got together all he had, set off for a distant country and there squandered his wealth in wild living. After he had spent everything, there was a severe famine in that whole country, and he began to be in need. So he went and hired himself out to a citizen of that country, who sent him to his fields to feed pigs. He longed to fill his stomach with the pods that the pigs were eating, but no one gave him anything.

"When he came to his senses, he said, 'How many of my father's hired men have food to spare, and here I am starving to death! I will set out and go back to my father and say to him: Father, I have sinned against heaven and against you. I am no longer worthy to be called your son; make me like one of your hired men.' So he got up and went to his father.

"But while he was still a long way off, his father saw him and was filled with compassion for him; he ran to his son, threw his arms around him and kissed him.

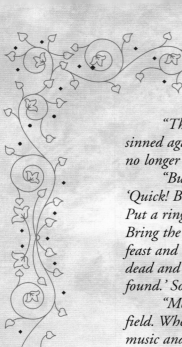

"The son said to him, 'Father, I have sinned against heaven and against you. I am no longer worthy to be called your son.'

"But the father said to his servants, 'Quick! Bring the best robe and put it on him. Put a ring on his finger and sandals on his feet. Bring the fattened calf and kill it. Let's have a feast and celebrate. For this son of mine was dead and is alive again; he was lost and is found.' So they began to celebrate.

"Meanwhile, the older son was in the field. When he came near the house, he heard music and dancing. So he called one of the servants and asked him what was going on. 'Your brother has come,' he replied, 'and your father has killed the fattened calf because he has him back safe and sound.'

"The older brother became angry and refused to go in. So his father went out and pleaded with him. But he answered his father, 'Look! All these years I've been slaving for you and never disobeyed your orders. Yet you never gave me even a young goat so I could celebrate with my friends. But when this son of yours who has squandered your property with prostitutes comes home, you kill the fattened calf for him!'

" 'My son,' the father said, 'you are always with me, and everything I have is yours. But we had to celebrate and be glad, because this brother of yours was dead and is alive again; he was lost and is found.' "

LUKE 15:11-32

My dad was very busy when I was a child, but I could always manage to get his attention. I can still see him sitting at his desk during my preschool years. He was in the final year of his doctoral studies at the University of Southern California, and the pressures were intense. Nevertheless, my brother and I took priority. I would climb on the chair behind him and spend a hour or two on his lap or even on his shoulders. He never seemed to mind. Every now and then he would stop to toss me in the air or play a game. These moments, even more than gifts and surprises, were the way he expressed genuine love to this wide-eyed child.

DANAE DOBSON

I know fame and power are for the birds. But then suddenly life comes into focus for me. And, ah, there stand my kids. I love them.

LEE IACOCCA

To me, champions are people who achieve their true purpose in life, who reach victory in many areas.

True champions measure themselves by a higher standard. Nobody's perfect. If we try to become champions by competing against imperfect people or measuring up to someone else's imperfect victories, we measure ourselves against imperfection. By accepting their weaknesses or failures, we keep ourselves from reaching our full potential. The only perfect man who ever walked this earth is Jesus Christ, God's Son. The champions I'm talking about compare themselves to Him and try to live up to the goals He sets. The best part is that He helps them do it. We don't need to compare ourselves with others or compete against them. To be true champions, we can measure ourselves against Him alone and compete against any force that would keep us from being like Him.

A. C. GREEN

> *When I was fourteen, my father was so ignorant I could hardly stand to have the old man around. But when I got to be twenty-one, I was astonished at how much he had learned in seven years.*
>
> **MARK TWAIN**

Ask the former
generations and find out what their
fathers learned,
for we were born only yesterday and know
nothing, and our days on earth are but a
shadow.
Will they not instruct you and tell you?
Will they not bring forth words from
their understanding?

JOB 8:8-10

We have the same passion for pens and tools and so you gave me many over the years. I think of you each time I use one of your gifts. (As you know, I prefer the pens because they don't skin my knuckles.) But you gave me a gift that is far more precious than pens or tools. That gift, Dad, is the gift of gentleness…the gift of having soft edges in a world that expects a man to be jagged and rough.

As I grow older I've begun to ask questions of older relatives. And I'm learning that your life as a son was rough and jagged. Your dad died when you were still young, and your mom, my grandmother, modeled a life of very rough edges.

But you came out of the experience not jagged, but gentle, not bitter but tender. Your gentleness is a package filled with awe and wonder. It's a supernatural gift that God gave you when he called you as his son and when you acknowledged him as your Heavenly Father. And now, both of you—my earthly and my heavenly Father, have passed on the gift of gentleness to me. I will eternally thank you for modeling for me, life with softened edges. Thanks, Dad. I LOVE YOU!

GARY RICHARDSON

A father has to be careful of his promises, because a real man will follow through.

A real man is a man of integrity. That means going all out in everything he does. When he says something, you can count on it, take it to the bank. If I say I'm going to do something, you can consider it done. The first time I violate that, my credibility is shot. Our reputations are only as good as our past performances

God is looking for men who will obey and be what he wants them to be.

MIKE SINGLETARY

I find that a good session of roughhousing one evening usually produces a happier child the next day.

S. ADAMS SULLIVAN

We run the risk of sounding trite by suggesting this, but this time in your life when your family is growing and changing has great potential for growth. One father, a high-level executive replaced during a corporate takeover, expressed this idea admirably. "I had been thinking recently that we needed to live more simply. I wondered if I would still be a serious follower of Jesus if my life had taken a decidedly poorer turn. Well, now we get to find out. And we get to find out if everything I've been telling my son about God's provision is what I really believe." Adapting to change can be terrifically stretching. We can become better people, better fathers, and better followers of Jesus.

JACK & JERRY SCHREUR

> *A family is a unit composed not only of children but of men, women, an occasional animal, and the common cold.*
>
> OGDEN NASH

The family you come from isn't as important as the family you're going to have.

RING LARDNER

It was late. I lay in my bed, perfectly still, straining so hard to hear that the silence roared in my ears. There it was . . . underneath the constant whir of the attic fan . . . just beyond the symphony of cicadas outside my bedroom window . . . across the hall. The low murmured tones of my father's voice. He was home, and the last conversation of the day was taking place. The darkness seemed to quiet the house.

A pause.

I imagined him sitting beside my mother on the edge of the bed. "Our heavenly Father," he began. And I knew it would all be there: my grades, Cynthia's braces, Marilyn's school-girl crush, the bills, the Holmans, the church, the missionaries. All whispered in a bedside prayer that was offered nightly throughout fifty years of marriage.

Then: "I love you, baby. You're a sweetheart."

"I love you, too, hon."

In that moment, the light of a thousand stars flooded my room, the bogeyman vanished, and angels danced on my dresser. I knew God Himself lived in our house! It was too much to bear.

STEPHEN HICKS

Bev and I had four children, and we would be the first to admit that they hampered our freedom, sapped our energy, and drained our bank account. But they were worth every bit of it! Children are a blessing, but a couple wrapped up in themselves and their activities will never enjoy "the little people."

TIM LAHAYE

My security was assured in many ways as a child. Every night I would go to the door of my room in my nightie and call out, "Papa, I'm ready for bed." He would come to my room and pray with me before I went to sleep. I can always remember that he took time with us and would tuck the blankets around my shoulders very carefully, with his own characteristic precision. Then he would put his hand gently on my face and say, "Sleep well, Corrie. I love you."

I sometimes remembered the feeling of my father's hand on my face. When I was lying beside Betsie on a wretched, dirty mattress in the dehumanizing prison, I would say, "O Lord, let me feel Your hand upon me."

CORRIE TEN BOOM

*hich of you fathers,
if your son asks for a fish, will give him a snake
instead? Or if he asks for an egg, will give him
a scorpion? If you then, though you are evil,
know how to give good gifts to your children,
how much more will your Father in heaven
give the Holy Spirit to those who ask him!"*

LUKE 11:11-13

Through his music, my father enjoyed more and more success every year, and life moved very fast. Yet, in the midst of all that was happening to him, I can't remember a single time when I felt I had to take the back seat to anything. I never once felt that I took second place to all that was going on in my parents' lives. Now, as a busy musician who's also a father, I realize even more clearly the value of time and the sparseness of it in life. It's the most priceless commodity that we have, and the fact that my parents always gave us their time first continues to amaze me.

DANN HUFF

Every parent is at some time the father of the unreturned prodigal, with nothing to do but keep his house open to hope.

JOHN CIARDI

A man of integrity is man enough to admit that he doesn't have all the answers. A man of integrity makes a promise intending to keep his word, even if it costs him dearly. A man of integrity admits failure and asks forgiveness when even his best intentions cannot or are not fulfilled; he picks himself up in the light of grace and forges ahead, learning from his defeats. A man of integrity is committed to the law of loving his neighbor as himself; whoever that neighbor happens to be. Most of all, a man of integrity loves Jesus Christ with passion, trusts Jesus Christ with fervor, and follows Jesus Christ with focused dedication.

Call your son to integrity. Invite him into the turbulent waters of faith as he grows up. Allow him to see you struggle with compromise and failure and arrogance and fear. Grant him permission to care for you when you are in need, without burdening him beyond what he can bear. Give him the gift of a father who is authentic, a dad who is more concerned with truth than personal acclaim. Pass on to your son the torch of faith in Jesus Christ, the "high priest whom we confess" (Hebrews 3:1).

STEVE LEE & CHAP CLARK

My father was a pastor, a missionary, and a church leader. Those who knew him would tell you that he was a great evangelist and church administrator with impeccable integrity and a heart for missions. To this day it is not unusual for someone to meet me for the first time, ask if I'm related to Dale Cryderman, and then say something like, "I came to God under his ministry."

Obviously, I am thankful for such a godly heritage, but what I appreciate most about my father was that he was the same man at home as he was in the pulpit: honest, compassionate, and kind. He taught me by example that the true measure of a man's success is the extent to which his actions live up to his words.

LYN CRYDERMAN

Young children are very active in the morning. They are well rested and alert. This often causes a problem for a parent or parents, who are also very active in the morning. When I was raising my children, this early morning time was the busiest of the day. This is even more true in contemporary family households, where breakfast time is often time for everyone to get ready to leave the house, for work or school or child care.

Because children are so alert at this hour, they are often more demanding. They remember questions they want to ask, comments they wish to make, and express a need for this, a need for that. Parents may think, "This isn't the time for all this nonsense. Can't these demands wait until we're more relaxed, later in the day?"

Children don't work that way. Young children are unable to shift their demands to a more "appropriate" time. Most demands are likely to surface when they're well rested and they can't be ignored or deferred. A child's concept of "later" is vastly different from the orderly place "later" holds for an adult.

> *He that raises a large family does, indeed, while he lives to observe them, stand a broader mark for sorrow; but then he stands a broader mark for pleasure too.*
>
> BENJAMIN FRANKLIN

Your first three minutes home from work or a business trip, followed by the next fifteen minutes, set the tone for the rest of the evening. As you arrive home, give a few quick honks in the driveway or garage to start the excitement, ring the doorbell several times, and add several unexpected spin-arounds to your ordinary hugs. Crucial tip: Don't sit down, pick up the paper, the phone or the mail until you've made contact individually with every family member.

PAUL LEWIS

I was standing with your daddy.
I guess I ought to warn you
        about him:
He is never without a
        quick as a flash retort
            filled with humor.
He will have you laughing a
            a hundred thousand times
        before he finally has to say,
            in answer to some preacher's question,
        "Her mother and I."
But for this moment,
        his mirth was gone,
            swallowed up
                by the deep sanctity of the miracle
            that had recently transpired
                before his very eyes.
"I have never seen anything
        quite like that before,"
were his quiet, reverent words.

I thought how right he was,
        remembering mornings
            in this very hospital
        when the birthings of children
            of my own,
                including Tom,
            had reconfirmed
                the miracle of life.

BOB BENSON

People talk about the emotions that come when a baby is born: exuberance, relief, giddiness, pure ecstasy; the thought that you have seen a miracle in front of your eyes.

I knew I was supposed to be feeling all of those things, and of course I did. But the dominant emotion inside me was a more basic one. I was scared; scared of what I knew was sure to come, and more scared about what I didn't know . . . I felt that a whole part of my life had just ended, been cut off, and I was beginning something for which I had no preparation.

BOB GREENE

Do not let your faults discourage you. Be patient with yourself as well as with your neighbor. Thinking too much will exhaust you and cause you to make a lot of mistakes. Learn to pray in all your daily situations. Speak, act, and talk as if you were in prayer. This is how you should live anyway.

Do everything without becoming too excited. As soon as you start to feel yourself getting too eager, quiet yourself before God. Listen to Him as He prompts you inwardly, then do only as He directs. If you do this, your words will be fewer but more effective. You will be calm, and good will be accomplished in greater measure.

I am not talking about continually trying to reason things out. Simply ask your Lord what He wants of you. This simple and short asking is better than your long-winded inner debates.

Turn toward God and it will be much easier to turn away from your strong natural feelings. Depend on the Lord within you. Your life will eventually become a prayer.

FRANCOIS FENELON

Thank you, Dad, for teaching me the value of getting up before the sun; for making breakfast every day for as many years as I lived at home; for working on Saturdays to ensure that our family of seven always had enough; for one of the most powerful memories of my youth—the unforgettable smells, accumulated on your clothes through a hard day's work at the shop; for teaching me the best way to wash a car; for Sundays that were set aside as days for worship and family; for providing us with a beautiful home, filled with memories; for still living in that home today and for its always welcoming, open door.

Thanks, Dad, for leaving an indelible mark on my life.

MIKE VANDERKLIP

How you prioritize your time and energy tells your son what matters most to you in life. If you spend most of your time working, your son will begin to understand that work is the most important thing in your life. If you spend most of your free time apart from your son, he will understand his place in your life.

I knew early on what my place was in my father's life. The way he allocated his time showed me exactly what was important . . . I knew that my dad thought I was important. I knew my place in his life was unassailable. I knew that his work, although very important to him, would never own his soul. I knew that I owned his soul and his heart. My father was committed to me and my brother, and he showed that commitment and built that commitment by investing his time and energy into our lives.

JACK & JERRY SCHREUR

"When Rachel was born, I saw her head come out. It looked misshapen. I was scared to death! I was afraid she was deformed." Brian Newman's fear evaporated instantly as he took the infant in his arms. She was not deformed; indeed, Rachel is an absolutely beautiful child; but had she not been, he still would have been full of joy. "I can't tell you the excitement of what it felt like to be there at delivery," he says. "Both times, I just cried. It's exhilarating. Breathtaking."

Brian Newman, a psychotherapist well in touch with his own feelings, articulates with great enthusiasm what many fathers know inside, even if they can't describe it. There is no substitute for being there from the beginning.

DR. FRANK MINIRTH
DR. BRIAN NEWMAN
DR. PAUL WARREN

> *Fathers, do not embitter your children, or they will become discouraged.*
>
> COLOSSIANS 3:21

For the small child, most theology is not learned by having it verbalized as much as by having parents live it out before him. I cannot tell my child that God will always listen to him if I'm preoccupied and will not listen. I cannot tell my child that God loves him if I am unloving and abrasive. I cannot tell my child that God cares if I don't. I must not say that God is always there if I'm never available.

Walking is talking. Without saying a word you speak volumes. Without uttering one sentence you present profound truths.

V. GILBERT BEERS

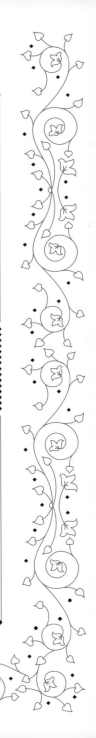

Now Israel's eyes were failing because of old age, and he could hardly see. So Joseph brought his sons close to him, and his father kissed them and embraced them.

Israel said to Joseph, "I never expected to see your face again, and now God has allowed me to see your children too."

Then he blessed Joseph and said, "May the God before whom my fathers Abraham and Isaac walked,
the God who has been my shepherd all my life to this day,
the Angel who has delivered me from all harm
—may he bless these boys.
May they be called by my name and the names of my fathers Abraham and Isaac,
and may they increase greatly upon the earth."

GENESIS 48:10-11, 15-16

From the time I was a child, my father pointed to Jesus as the ultimate role model. Whenever he would enjoy success or suffer adversity, he would look to Christ's example as the way to face life. Jesus humbled himself and became a servant leader instead of using his power and superiority to control others. He led his disciples to walk in truth, love, and humility. I have tried to follow this example, even though I know I can never be perfect. My dad pointed me to the greatest role model I could find. Knowing that I have a loving Heavenly Father to whom I can turn in prayer whenever I need help has made all the difference in my life. I also can count on my earthly dad to forgive me when I fail and love me no matter what.

LT. JOHN MATUSZAK, JR.

Many parents teach their children to assert themselves, to "insist upon their rights." This is certainly an important lesson, but it is an incomplete one. Most children are never taught that rights are accompanied by responsibilities; if we have a right, we also have an obligation to act in accommodation to others. Many children, asserting their rights, grow up to be rude in their actions at best, criminal at worst.

What parents do more than anything else in nurturing children is to give them values. True, they provide food for a healthy body and teach fundamentals for physical safety, but more than any of these things, their greatest and longest lasting effect upon their children is in the values they impart. Parents teach these values in informal oral lessons, but, most of all, they teach values by example. A parent who, in the presence of a child, admits to the store clerk, "You gave me a dollar too much in change," is teaching values. A parent, speeding down the freeway with an eye in the rearview mirror looking for the highway patrol, is teaching values to his child in the back seat. A parent who cheats on his income tax and brags about it at a neighborhood barbecue is telling his child that ethics are for losers.

O f all nature's
gifts to the human
race, what is sweeter to a man
than his children?

CICERO

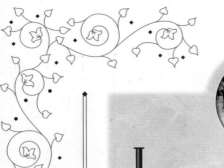

I want my children to enter into the delights of life with enthusiasm. I want them to appreciate their God-given senses, to enjoy the beauties of His handiwork, to be grateful for the scent of the rose or the taste of pancakes on a winter morning. I want them to delight in taking their own children out in the forest to appreciate the leaves and wildflowers, the birds and woodland creatures, to gaze in awe at the clouds in the sky, to be delighted with the sunset and the harvest moon rising in the autumn sky. I want my children to enthusiastically impart these values to their children and thereby impart an affinity with the Creator through the enjoyment of His footprints and fingerprints.

V. GILBERT BEERS

Formal training can never take the place of family living.

DAVID JEREMIAH

I realized intensely that, like Tom, I wish to be a father to Matthew and Jason until the day I die and that my fathering is not limited by time and, perhaps, not even by death. This is a comforting thought, and it also makes parenting seem a far more permanent and important thing than this notion, which our culture sometimes seems to endorse, of temporary caretaking.

RICHARD LOUV

A h! what would the world be to us
    If the children were no more?
    We should dread the desert behind us
    Worse than the dark before.

HENRY WADSWORTH LONGFELLOW

The best way to make children good is to make them happy.

OSCAR WILDE

We can choose to look at our fathers and see the good things that they have passed on to us. We can sift through our childhood and find the things they have taught us that are worth passing down to our own children. Our heritage can become a source of joy and strength instead of a source of shame. It is useless to pretend that our fathering is not influenced by the way we were fathered. Whether we realize it or not, it is probably the most powerful influence of our fathering styles.

JACK & JERRY SCHREUR

H is father would say sometimes, when he was in the midst of the comforts of this life, 'All this, and heaven too!'"

MATTHEW HENRY

Carl and Ivy Jefferson had it made. Well, not exactly. They used to have it made, until Ivy was stricken by peritonitis. She spent over nine weeks in the hospital, at a time when Carl's business particularly demanded his attention . . . Carl had to quit traveling. He had to give up a lot of his field work, and with it went a lot of his income.

Carl chafed . . . here he sat around the house, coloring pictures with the preschool Cathy and waiting for Janey to walk in the door from second grade. And Ivy so sick . . . Life had turned gray.

Here Janey came up the sidewalk. She slammed the front door. Carl had pulled her fine, dark hair up into a neat ponytail this morning. Now the ponytail hung in disarray, with flyaway wispies sticking out all over. Her clothes were a disaster too—a big smudge on her shirt, grass stains, and a rip in the knees of her jeans. Another successful day at school, obviously.

"Is Mommy home yet?"

"Not yet, Sugar. Next week maybe." Carl gave her a hug . . .

She clung, so he clung. "Promise you won't get mad at me, Daddy?"

"What kind of question is that? Okay. I promise."

"Don't get mad at me for saying this, okay? I'm sorry Mommy's sick. I don't mean I like Mommy being sick. But I'm glad you're home. It's so great! This is the best time I ever had in my life."

DR. FRANK MINIRTH
DR. BRIAN NEWMAN
DR. PAUL WARREN

Immediate openings
For an honorable job,
With long hours
No time off—
Must be willing to work all hours,
Including the middle of the night,
Weekends, holidays, and vacations.
Requires survival traits,
Like strength and patience,
Imagination, humor, and flexibility,
Intelligence and understanding,
And above all, a good heart.
Must be a human being,
Kind and gentle,
With basic goodness and fearlessness.
Leadership qualities are necessary,
And the ability to instruct and guide
      is a requirement.
Receive on-the-job training,
With no pay.
There will be unpredictable surprises
      and rewards—
Like joy, love, pain, fun, and many
      difficulties.
Want a challenge?
Be a dad!

Children are our most valuable natural
resource.

HERBERT HOOVER

I am becoming right now the father that I will be for the rest of my son's life. It's these next fifteen years that will be my fatherhood to him. Certainly, after he grows up . . . I'll still be around, hopefully, and still be there for what I can offer at that time. But the daddy that I will be imparting to him is being done now.

My challenge is to make it happen now. I feel great pressure in the sense that there's no making it up . . . I've got a certain number of years to get it all in, and then the boy is going to grow up and has got to have the tools to go on with it. I can't always be there: I might die. I might fall on times when I can't help him, so I've got to give him that stuff, whatever that "father stuff" is, I've got to give it now.

I'll always be Ken. But the father my children take with them, when they get up in the morning and drive to work, come home and become fathers, will be the daddy I am now. That daddy will be inside of my sons.

KEN

We find delight in the beauty and happiness of children that makes the heart too big for the body.

RALPH WALDO EMERSON

Last night my little boy confessed to me
Some childish wrong;
And kneeling at my knee
He prayed with tears—
"Dear God, make me a man
Like Daddy—wise and strong;
I know you can."

Then while he slept
I knelt beside his bed,
Confessed my sins,
And prayed with low-bowed head.
"O God, make me a child
Like my child here—
Pure, guileless,
Trusting Thee with faith sincere."

ANDREW GILLIES

One day, Charles Adams, son of John Quincy Adams, entered these words into his diary: Went fishing with my son—a day wasted.

His son, Brook Adams, also kept a diary, which is still in existence. On the same day he wrote: Went fishing with my father—the most wonderful day of my life!

CHRIS HALVERSON

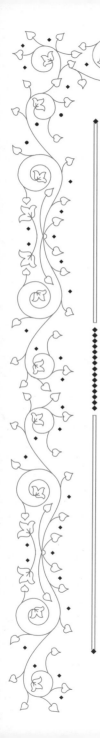

Why don't we teach young boys that fatherhood makes you high? Why do we transmit to them news mainly of breadwinning and the chores, and ignore the spiritual transport, the blisteringly beautiful moments of fatherhood?

Are we embarrassed to talk about this?

Fathers, when invited to talk about these things, often described blinding moments of realization: sitting with their sons or daughters in their arms and suddenly realizing that they would do anything—lay down their lives, jump in front of a car, anything—to protect their children. Or they described walking with their child or looking at him or her in the rearview mirror, and suddenly realizing this is my child and feeling an overwhelming sense of awe. And at these instants of the spirit, tears came to their eyes.

RICHARD LOUV

New York's nonprofit Manpower Demonstration Research Corporation, which funds counseling programs in eleven cities, asks fathers to write obituaries for themselves in the voices of their children, as if their children were writing them. I wonder: What would my obituary say, if Jason or Matthew were to write it? What would your children write?

RICHARD LOUV

History shows that at the beginning of every major revival, there has been a fresh realization of mankind's self-centered ways. When people finally understand how deeply they're concerned about pleasing themselves and how little they care about pleasing God, they begin to fall on their knees in repentance and seek each other's forgiveness. Almost immediately they go to their brothers and sisters, people in their churches, people in their neighborhoods and towns, and seek reconciliation. It's such a stunning supernatural turn of events that it pierces to the heart of any community. And then the dam breaks, releasing a great torrent of God's grace and power.

It's time for a group of bold men to say, "I've had enough of this love affair with myself. I'm going to repent . . . Even if no one else does it, I'm going to do it anyway. It has to start somewhere, so let it start with me. I'll admit it. I am self-centered. I want to confess that to God and to you. Will you forgive me, Lord? Will you forgive me, my wife, my children?"

Will you be one of those men?

GARY SMALLEY & JOHN TRENT

It had been a day filled with trouble. Everything had gone wrong. In the mood of defeat, I sought the refuge and comfort of home.

As I turned into the lane, a glorious sunset compelled me to stop. The entire western half of the sky was a vast canvas tinted as only God can paint. The heavens were telling the glory of God.

My soul was suddenly drenched with wonder. People and plans may fail, I thought, but God's constancy remains.

Trouble and victory were constant companions of Jesus. When it was sunset for His earthly life, He took the colors of His love and the brush of His faith and painted those forbidding clouds with glory—eternal victory.

Should we expect life for us to be different from His? He said, "You will find trouble in the world." But He immediately added a note of encouragement and victory: "Never lose heart, I have conquered the world." So can we—with his help.

CECIL P. HARDIN

Dear God, thank You for Your constant presence in my life. I am humbled when I consider that the Sovereign of the universe cares enough to rejoice over me and quiet me with His love.

I also marvel at Your provision for me. Because Your strength is unlimited, my inner well never has to be empty. Your strength is artesian, constantly surging up to exactly what I need in every moment. You give me supernatural wisdom that supersedes my knowledge. You provide emotional equipoise when I am under pressure. You engender resoluteness in my will and vision when my responsibilities become demanding.

Father, quiet my heart with Your unqualified, indefatigable love. Provide me with confidence, security, and peace. Enable me to have absolute trust in Your faithfulness. You make me stable and secure. Nothing can separate me from Your love in Christ. Whatever I go through today will be used to deepen my relationship with You and help me grow in Your grace.

LLOYD JOHN OGILVIE

For the next seven days in a row, make "I love you" the first and last words you say each day to your wife and children.

PAUL LEWIS

All in vain is splendid preaching, and the noble things we say.

All our talk is wasted teaching if we do not lead the way.

We can never by reviewing all the sermons on the shelves,

Keep the younger hands from doing what we often do ourselves.

AUTHOR UNKNOWN

It was a cold, rainy night. My son Gordon, now thirty-eight years old but then twenty-one, finally came home around 1:00 A.M. after a long night of smoking marijuana with his friends. I was livid, embarrassed, distraught, and afraid. How could this young man whom we loved so much do this to his mother and me? It wasn't fair; it wasn't right. It was happening to other parents, but who would have ever thought it would have reared its ugly head in the Engstrom family.

We couldn't understand why. But this particular evening I held my peace, even though I had a mind to give Gordon a tongue lashing he would never forget. I listened to him as he shouted that most Christians were phonies, the church was filled with hypocrites, and there were at least a hundred ways to God. On and on he went.

The more I listened, the more something began to happen inside me. After a while, I no longer saw a son whose head was clouded from the effects of pot. Instead, I began to hear him. Even though I didn't—and don't—approve of anyone's ingesting drugs for recreational purposes, I knew that much of what Gordon had to say was true. There is a tremendous absence of love for each other within the body of Christ. Too often our lifestyles do bear little resemblance to that of the Man from Galilee. And yes, Christians are not perfect, and no, they don't all know how to be friends.

I can remember a hot tear falling on my cheek, then another and another as Gordon spoke. I knew in my heart of hearts he was also talking about me. I only tell you this story to say this: Although that evening was difficult, humiliating, and upsetting, I think it may have been the first night I really listened to Gordon. In a fresh, new way, I was establishing a real relationship with my son. It was something that changed my life—our lives. It was the beginning of what has now become a beautiful friendship.

TED ENGSTROM

The smile, of course, is amazing. Just a few days ago I was so moved to see it for the first time. Now she is doing it all the time. I will pick her up and say something to her, and her whole face will light up. I will be talking, and the sound of a word will apparently please her, and this toothless grin will just spread over her face. Today I squeezed her foot and said "foot." It was as if I had told her the most hilarious joke in the world. When the smile went away I said "foot" again. Again, that smile. And again and again.

She will never remember any of this, of course. And I will never forget.

BOB GREENE

Fatherhood is pretending the present you love most is soap-on-a-rope.

BILL COSBY

Rise up, O men of God!
Have done with lesser things.
Give heart and mind and soul and
    strength
To serve the King of kings.

Rise up, O men of God!
The kingdom tarries long.
Bring in the day of brotherhood
And end the night of wrong.

Rise up, O men of God!
The church for you doth wait,
Her strength unequal to her task;
Rise up and make her great!

Lift high the cross of Christ!
Tread where His feet have trod.
As brothers of the Son of Man,
Rise up, O men of God!

WILLIAM P. MERRILL

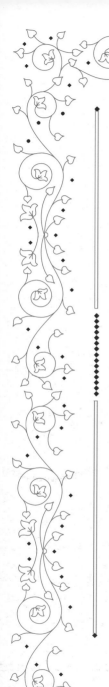

I had finally had it. The children were loud, cranky, impossible. I was tired and fed up. My wife was tired and fed up. I decided that I was going to run away from it all and have a day just for me. I wanted to spoil myself. I wanted to have a day in which I did just what I wanted to do. I was going to live it up and be as greedy as I pleased. I wasn't going to tend to anyone except myself.

I zoomed out of the house with fifty dollars. There! I did it! I said to myself as I drove to the highway and headed north.

Well, I drove to a mall and had a wild time in a bookstore and bought the collected poems of Walt Whitman. After that I drove and drove to a McDonald's and ordered two hamburgers, my own large fries, and my own large soda. I ate everything without being interrupted, without giving my pickle to anyone, without wiping someone's mouth, nose, lap. Then I bought the biggest chocolate ice cream I could find.

I was free. I was out on the town, so I drove to a movie theater and watched a movie without buying popcorn, without someone sitting on my lap, without escorting someone to the bathroom. I was a free man. I was living it up. And I was miserable.

By the time I had returned home, everyone was asleep. As I slipped into bed, my wife whispered, "We missed you."

"Me, too," I answered. I never ran away from home again.

If you are in the middle of the pressures of raising a family, remember, it's no fun being alone.

"Children are a reward from the Lord," wrote the psalmist. So take the kids today to McDonald's, or to a bookstore, or to the movies. Take them anywhere except out of your heart.

CHRISTOPHER DE VINCK

H

e will turn the hearts of the fathers to their children, and the hearts of the children to their fathers.

MALACHI 4:6

The amazing thing is that when I hold my baby daughter—in her little white suit tonight, with the tiny rosebuds all over it—and I think about how she has become the central thing in our lives, and has changed everything, I have to think twice before I realize that as important as she is, she weighs just over seven pounds. So small, so fragile.

BOB GREENE

The danger of burnout is very real to me. When I become too busy, there is little time to be refueled by Your love, joy, peace, and patience. I start living on my own resources and forget that You are the source of wisdom, knowledge, discernment, vision, and the power to lead others. I never was meant to make it on my own. Forgive me for trying.

LLOYD JOHN OGILVIE

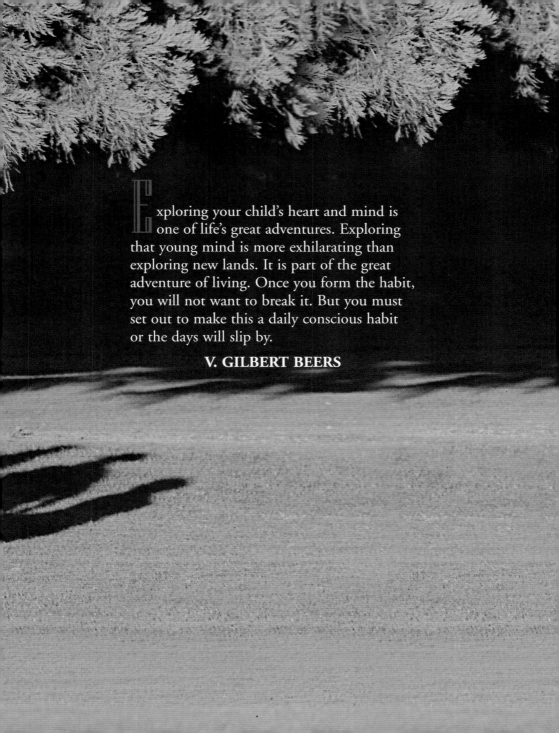

Exploring your child's heart and mind is one of life's great adventures. Exploring that young mind is more exhilarating than exploring new lands. It is part of the great adventure of living. Once you form the habit, you will not want to break it. But you must set out to make this a daily conscious habit or the days will slip by.

V. GILBERT BEERS

They were standing there—my father with a camera in his hand, my mother carrying a bag full of presents—and they made their hellos to Susan and me. They walked into the living room. I don't think they were expecting to see our baby Amanda yet, but she was on her back asleep in the carriage there.

They made sounds that I can only describe as animal-like when they saw her. The sight seemed to touch something so basic in them that the sounds came out; it was as if something had squeezed their hearts. I realized instantly that nothing I may ever accomplish in the world of work will possibly affect them in the way the sight of their granddaughter did.

BOB GREENE

In the brief years of my own fatherhood, I have realized that when I am fathering I feel more like a man than at any other time in my life. To say this is not to presume that I am satisfied with my fathering—we live in an age when many men sense that fatherhood can be the most mysterious and fulfilling journey that a man can make—but we find ourselves struggling to define the terms, feeling somehow that we have yet to find the essence of our fatherhood.

RICHARD LOUV

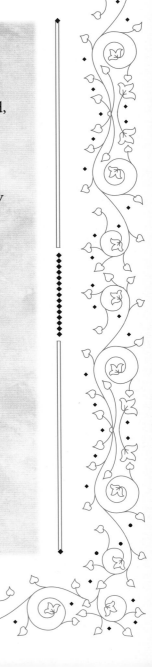

To laugh often and love much; to win the respect of intelligent persons and affection of children; to earn the approbation of honest critics and to endure the betrayal of a false friend; to appreciate beauty; to find the best in others; to give of one's self; to leave the world a bit better, whether by a healthy child, a garden patch, or a redeemed social condition; to have played and laughed with exultation; to know that even one life has breathed easier because you have lived— this is to have succeeded.

RALPH WALDO EMERSON

My daughter is ten years old. Seven years ago I was between jobs. I was her day-care provider; her mom worked, and her siblings were in school. I was desperate. I had just finished getting an advanced degree, but I couldn't find a job doing what I wanted to do. I was working as a handyman; I was driving a taxicab; and I was miserable because I wasn't fitting the role of being a breadwinner. But if you listen to my daughter today, she'll sit there and wax poetic about riding around town in Dad's big yellow cab when she was three years old. Or she'll describe the jobs that she went out on with me when I was building fences and painting. Or the time that we were going to take the trolley to Tijuana and we got lost, ending up in Santee, many miles away. It was a great adventure for her. That was the focal point of her young life.

JON CONNOR

The fingernails are the thing. Everything about the baby is amazing, but when I look at her fingernails—so small you couldn't even measure them on a ruler, but perfectly formed—that's when the miracle hits home again every time.

BOB GREENE

The most important thing a father can do for his children is to love their mother.

THEODORE M. HESBURGH

I am God's shepherd for my child,
put here to supply all his needs.
I help my child lie down
where he will be safe and secure,
and I lead him to quiet,
untroubled places
where his soul will be restored.

I guide my child in paths of righteousness
for God's sake and his own.
Even when my child walks through
dark and difficult places,
he does not need to be afraid,
because I am with him, and
that comforts him.

I provide all the good food my child needs,
even when his "friends" who want
to hurt him are nearby.
I treat him like a young prince or
princess,
and bring a rich family heritage to
him.

As long as my child lives,
I will always be his friend,
sharing kindness and good things.
I will be a leader and role model for
my child,
so that at the end of life we will
live together in God's heavenly
home.

V. GILBERT BEERS

Every time I am away from my infant daughter Amanda for even a night, it's a giddy feeling to see her again. I walked in and she was drooling down her chin and onto her clothes; I asked Susan if she could be getting a cold or something.

But Susan said that, according to all the books, this is normal; it's increased salivation, which is a prelude to teething. Apparently we're in for a long spell of Amanda spitting all over us—after which she will begin cutting tiny teeth.

I'm glad to know that now, because I'm going to spend that much more time concentrating on watching her smile. There's something about her smile with no teeth that I love; maybe it's that it somehow defines her being a baby. Once the teeth come in, she'll still be little, but not quite so much an infant.

The shoulders of my shirt are sopping wet. Amanda just laughs and drools on me some more.

BOB GREENE

W hile I'm carrying my son around with me on errands, someone may pause to admire, asking if I'm babysitting today. That automatically triggers a kind of slow, smoldering sizzle in my gut. Usually, I just let it pass. But I don't forget it. It makes me just boil. I'm not a babysitter. I'm a father!"

"STEVE" AS QUOTED BY KYLE D. PRUETT

May I urge you as fathers of young children, whether compliant or strong-willed, to provide for them an unshakable faith in Jesus Christ. This is your most important function, fathers. How can anything else compare in significance to the goal of keeping the family circle unbroken in the life to come? What an incredible objective to work toward!

If the salvation of our children is really that vital to us, then our spiritual training should begin before children can even comprehend what it is all about. They should grow up seeing their parents on their knees before God, talking to Him. They will learn quickly at that age and will never forget what they've seen and heard. Even if they reject their faith later, the remnant of it will be with them for the rest of their lives.

JAMES C. DOBSON

> *Fathers, do not exasperate your children; instead, bring them up in the training and instruction of the Lord.*
>
> **EPHESIANS 6:4**

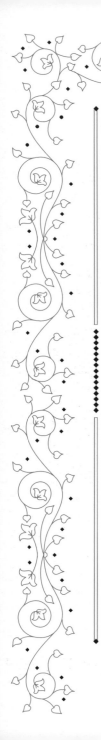

Somewhere I heard about a father-to-be who spent his evenings fixing a bedroom to become the nursery and in painting, papering, getting new furniture, and helping his wife get life's little necessities in order for the soon-to-come-on-the-scene new baby.

"You're spending all your spare time getting ready for the new baby, aren't you?" a friend remarked.

"Yes," said the father. "I've never before spent so much time getting the house ready for a person I've never met."

Already in this father's and mother's mind they were thinking of their baby-to-be as an important person. And they should. A new baby is one of the most important VIP's on earth, a brand-new person who has joined the world scene and will soon leave footprints (handprints, too, some with jam and peanut butter) all over it.

V. GILBERT BEERS

We took our son Eric too much for granted. Perhaps we all take each other too much for granted. The routines of life distract us; our own pursuits make us oblivious; our anxieties and sorrows, unmindful. The beauties of the familiar go unremarked. We do not treasure each other enough.

He was a gift to us for twenty-five years. When the gift was finally snatched away, I realized how great it was. Then I could not tell him. An outpouring of letters arrived, many expressing appreciation for Eric. They all made me weep again: each word of praise a stab of loss.

How can I be thankful, in his goneness, for what he was? I find I am. But the pain of the no more outweighs the gratitude of the once was. Will it always be so?

I didn't know how much I loved him until he was gone.

NICHOLAS WOLTERSTORFF

It was the middle of the night when Kris called my name. I heard her first "Daddy!" immediately and sprang out of bed and down the hall to her room. She was in distress. There had been a bad dream, and Kris was having a rough time sorting out what was real and what was part of the dream.

Why had she called her father? Because her instinct somehow told her that when equilibrium is in jeopardy, fathers can help restore balance. Her young mind had set up a pattern of responses to uneasy situations: call for Dad; he knows how to make upside down things turn right side up again.

GORDON MACDONALD

> *I have no greater joy than to hear that my children are walking in the truth.*
>
> 3 JOHN 4

When you're holding your baby and she's falling asleep in your arms slowly and the evening is slipping away and your mind is racing through the thousand things at the top of your list, and you begin to feel—as all fathers and all mothers inevitably begin to feel from time to time—that you're wasting your time taking care of this little kid, try to remember that next year you won't be able to hold her in the same way, she won't go to sleep in your arms, and after a few more years you'll be happy to get a hug on the run. Our children are here to stay, but our babies and toddlers and preschoolers are gone as fast as they can grow up—and we have only a short moment with each.

S. ADAMS SULLIVAN

Every night after dinner we put Amanda in her crib and let her squirm around and look at the mobiles. The high scream she has developed is almost constant when she does this. It is clearly not a scream of pain; it is almost like a long, continuous laugh, and when we hear it we know she's having a good time.

So tonight we were watching television and talking, and we heard that happy scream from the other room.

"You know, we should really pay attention when we hear that," Susan said. "This is the only time in her life that she's going to be allowed to just lie there and scream out for joy."

And it's true; things are bound to get so complicated, and so soon. Before long she will begin to have people's problems instead of just babies' problems.

I got up and turned the sound down on the TV set. And we sat on the couch, listening to all that joy from the other room.

BOB GREENE

Not long ago Sarah, my seven-year-old daughter, and I tasted the "sweetness" of the Word together. She had shown considerable interest in reading at school and I asked if she would be interested in reading directly from the Bible to me on a regular basis. We would use her own Bible and examine a paragraph at a time. She became excited by the idea, ran into her bedroom to get her Bible, and what began as a father-daughter experiment in Bible reading has now become a family custom. We look forward to our reading, and I have often experienced a sense of God's presence and felt the Holy Spirit illuminate the passage as Sarah reads it. It "tastes good."

DENNIS FISHER

As I grew up, I never felt overwhelmed with advice. I felt respected, even when I did dumb things. Once, when I was perhaps seventeen, I became enraged with our youth leader over what I regarded as his narrowly legalistic attitude in a certain matter. Our debate turned into a heated yelling match that ended when I hurled a hymnbook across the room in his direction, stomped out the door, and drove home. I knew I was wrong.

When I walked into our house, Dad was on the phone with the man I had assaulted, listening to a tirade against me. I wondered what Dad would do. I heard him end the phone conversation with something like, "Sounds as if he didn't handle things very well, but I'm glad he has spunk enough to have real convictions." He hung up, turned to me, and calmly asked what had happened. He listened as I presented a terribly biased account of the incident, and then he commented on the importance of handling convictions responsibly. That was it. He went on with his evening and I felt respected. I also resolved to express my convictions in a more godly fashion.

LAWRENCE J. CRABB, JR.

The deep knee bend is a father's basic exercise. It gives a man with small kids the wherewithal to get close to his children—right down on their level. Leaning over doesn't have the same effect—it means that you are coming from somewhere else.

You know how happy your child is when you lift him up to the level of your face. It's not all in the exhilaration of being lifted; a lot of the pleasure is simply in being on your level. Nearly the same result can be achieved with a deep squat to your child's level.

A regimen of deep knee bends is a simple physical way to work on closing the generation gap between you and your kids. There's not much room for confusion and misunderstanding between people who can look each other in the eye while they're talking. And if you get in shape to bob down to your child's level regularly, you'll start to see the world from her vantage point, which can't help but give you a better appreciation of where she's coming from.

S. ADAMS SULLIVAN

Fathers are no longer, if they ever were, merely a biological necessity—a social accident. They are an important influence on their children's development. And a close relationship between father and child benefits the father as well as the child. Children need their fathers, but fathers need their children too.

ROSS D. PARKE

A little child, a limbering elf, singing, dancing to itself…make such a vision to the sight, as fills a father's eyes with light.

SAMUEL TAYLOR COLERIDGE

If you have a family and you love them, you are rich, but don't forget to enrich them as well by making sure that the love you have in your heart is felt by each and every member of your family at the deepest level of their lives.

Communicate that love to them now; don't wait for the difficult times. Make sure the love bond is strong and the cords are woven tight.

DAVID JEREMIAH

Life is difficult, but it is also an adventure—and an exciting one at that. I'm persuaded in my own life that God's calling demands steady, unmoved perseverance. This lesson—a lesson that lies at the heart of Christian discipleship—is one that I learned from a father whose wisdom in dealing with a rebellious son opened my heart to hear the call of God, "Come, follow me."

DR. ROBERT WEBBE

I am not too concerned that my family remember me as a profound person, but rather as a husband and father who was fun to live with. I really do not care if they're able to repeat rules and regulations that came from my lips, but I hope they never forget the sound of my laughter. I hope it is absorbed in the walls of my home. That's one particular contribution I desire very much to make permanent.

CHARLES R. SWINDOLL

May the
Lord, the Maker of heaven
and earth, bless you.

PSALM 134:3

SOURCES

V. Gilbert Beers, *Best Friends for Life* (Harvest House Publishers: Eugene, OR) 1988.

Bob Benson, *Laughter in the Walls,* (Gaither Family Resources: Alexandria, IN) 1990.

Corrie ten Boom, *In My Father's House* (Fleming H. Revell: Old Tappan, NJ) 1976.

Jon Connor, quoted in Richard Louv, *Father Love* (Pocket Books, a division of Simon & Schuster: New York, NY) 1993.

Christopher de Vinck, *Simple Wonders* (Zondervan Publishing House: Grand Rapids, MI) 1995.

James C. Dobson, *Parenting Isn't for Cowards* (Word Publishers: Waco, TX) 1987.

James C. Dobson, Sr., in Gloria Gaither, *What My Parents Did Right* (Star Song Publishing Group: Nashville, TN) 1991.

Ted Engstrom, with Robert C. Larson, *The Fine Art of Friendship* (Thomas Nelson Publishers: Nashville, TN) 1985.

Dennis Fisher, "Jewish Lessons for Disciplining Children" (*Discipleship Journal,* no. 30, page 40) 1985.

A. C. Green, *Victory* (Creation House: Mary Lake, FL) 1994.

Bob Greene, *Good Morning, Merry Sunshine* (Atheneum: New York, NY) 1984.

Chris Halverson, *"Perspective"* (Father's Day, Concern Ministries, Inc.: Box 7800, McLean, VA 22106-7800) 1998.

Cecil P. Hardin, *100 Meditations on Hope* (The Upper Room: Nashville, TN) 1995.

Lee Iacocca in *365 Reflections on Fathers* (Adams Media Corporation: Holbrook, MA) 1998.

David Jeremiah, *Exposing the Myths of Parenthood* (Word Publishing: Dallas, TX) 1988.

Tim LaHaye, *The Battle for the Family* (Fleming H. Revell: Old Tappan, NJ) 1982.

Steven Lee & Chap Clark, *Boys to Men* (Moody Press: Chicago, IL) 1995.

Kevin Leman, *Bringing Up Kids Without Tearing Them Down* (Delacorte Press: New York, NY) 1993.

Paul Lewis, *A Dad After God's Own Heart* (Warner Press, Inc.: Anderson, IN) 1995.

Richard Louv, *Father Love* (Pocket Books, a division of Simon & Schuster: New York, NY) 1993.

Max Lucado, *God Came Near* (Questar Publishers: Sisters, OR) 1987.

Gordon MacDonald, *The Effective Father* (Tyndale House Publishers: Wheaton, IL) 1977.

William P. Merrill, *"Rise Up, O Men of God,"* 1911.

Dr. Frank Minirth, Dr. Brian Newman, Dr. Paul Warren, *The Father Book* (Thomas Nelson Publishers, Inc.: Nashville, TN) 1992.

David Moore, *Five Lies of the Century* (Tyndale House Publishers: Wheaton, IL) 1995.

Andrew Murray, *How to Raise Your Children for Christ*, public domain.

Lloyd John Ogilvie, *One Quiet Moment* (Harvest House Publishers: Eugene, OR) 1997.

Ross D. Parke, *Fathers* (Harvard University Press: Cambridge, MA) 1981.

Kyle D. Pruett, M.D., *The Nurturing Father* (Warner Books: New York: NY) 1987.

Theodore Roosevelt, in *Theodore Roosevelt's Letter to His Children* (Charles Scribner's Sons: New York, NY) 1919, 1947.

Jack & Jerry Schreur, *Fathers & Sons* (Victor Books: Wheaton, IL) 1995.

Gary Smalley & John Trent, *The Hidden Value of a Man* (Focus on the Family: Colorado Springs, CO) 1992.

Charles Stanley, *A Man's Touch* (Chariot Victor Books: Colorado Springs, CO) 1977.

S. Adams Sullivan, *The Father's Almanac* (Doubleday & Company: Garden City, NY) 1980.

Charles R. Swindoll, *Living on the Ragged Edge* (Word Publishing, Inc.: Waco, TX) 1985.

Nicholas Wolterstorff, *Lament for a Son* (William B. Eerdmans Publishing: Grand Rapids, MI) 1987.

PHOTO CREDITS

12: Stock Market, New York: Lance Nelson
13: Stock Market, New York: Joe Battor
15,81,89,90: Stock Market, New York: Paul Barton
18: Stock Market, New York: Jim Earickson
23,66,110: Stock Market, New York: Tom & DeAnn McCarthy
25: Stock Market, New York: C/B Productions
26,67: Westlight: Craig Aurness
30: Stock Market: Pete Saloutos
33,123: Stock Market: Tom Stewart
35: Comstock
39, 125: Westlight: Julie Habel
41: Westlight: Michael Pole
42: Westlight: Doug Wilson
48: Stock Market: George Disario
53: Westlight: Walter Hodges
69, 72: Stock Market: Roy Marsh
78: Stock Market: Jose L. Pelaez
83: Stock Market: Peter Beck
85: Comstock
95: Stock Market: Ronnie Kaufman
98: Westlight: Ken Redding
106: Westlight: R.V. Jones
121: Stock Market: Trudi Unger